Sophie & The French Magician

At The Fair

One day Sophie went to a fair with her parents and they saw a French magician.

The magician greeted everyone with **Bonjour**. This means hello in French.

Then he said in French that his name was Luc.

For his first trick, the French magician put three boxes on a table. He placed a coin in one of the boxes and then told everyone to clap and count to three in French.

(Now the magician needs as much help as possible, so if you're reading this story now, please join in too!)

Then they all had to guess which box the coin was in!

Sophie watched in amazement. It wasn't in **un**.
It wasn't in **deux**. And it *wasn't* in **trois**!

The coin had disappeared!

For his next trick, he asked everyone to clap
and say three times, **un lapin**.

Sophie's mum whispered to her that **un lapin**
was the French word for a rabbit.

And then suddenly out of his hat came…….

un lapin

Next the French magician got out his wand.

He told everyone to clap and say three times
un oiseau.

Sophie's mum whispered to her
that **un oiseau** was the French
word for a bird.

Suddenly **un oiseau** appeared on the table!

How had he done that? It was amazing!

Next he turned to Sophie and he asked:

Sophie realised that **animal préféré**
meant favourite animal. So she
replied **un chien** as her favourite
animal was a dog. Surely he couldn't
make **un chien** appear!

This time, he had a very long balloon in his hand.
He asked the crowd to join in with him as he said:

un chien   un chien   U N   C H I E N

And then suddenly the balloon turned into….

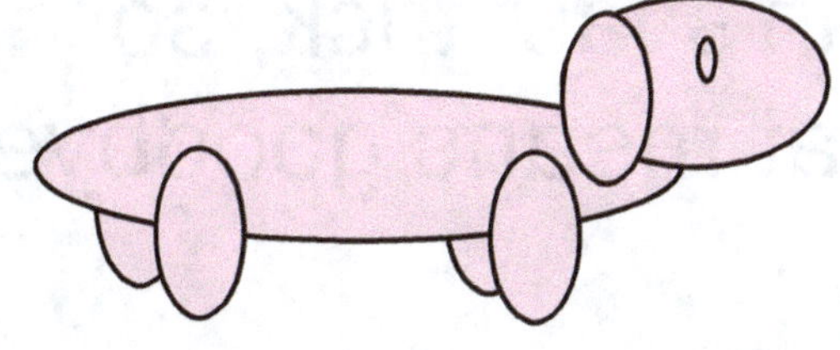

un chien

It had been so much fun watching the French magician! For his final trick he placed his hat on the floor and he asked everyone to say **bonbons** three times as they clapped:

And out of the hat came **des bonbons** - lots and lots of delicious looking sweets! That was really amazing! Everyone thanked the French magician by saying "**Merci.**"

That was the French magician's last trick, so they all said "**Au revoir**". That means goodbye in French.

Sophie & The French Magician

Sophie's Birthday Party

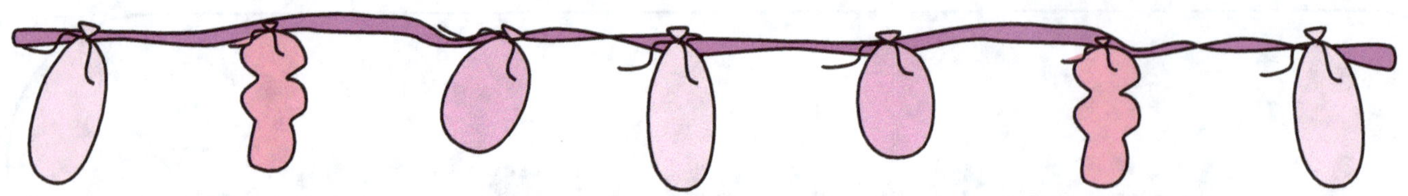

It was Sophie's birthday, and the French magician arrived at her birthday party!

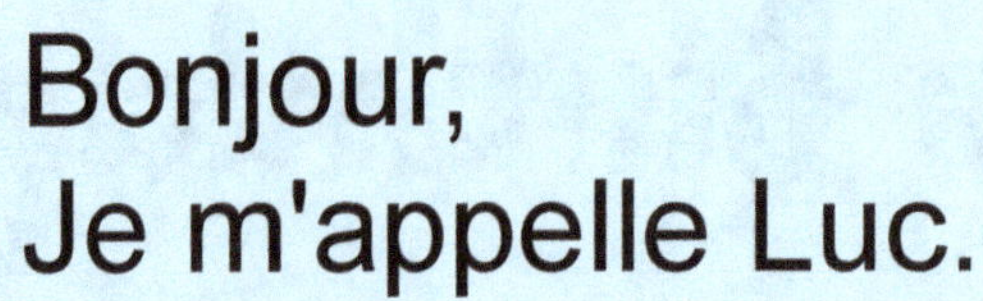

The French magician said hello in French. Then he said that his name was Luc.

Sophie introduced herself in French to the French magician.

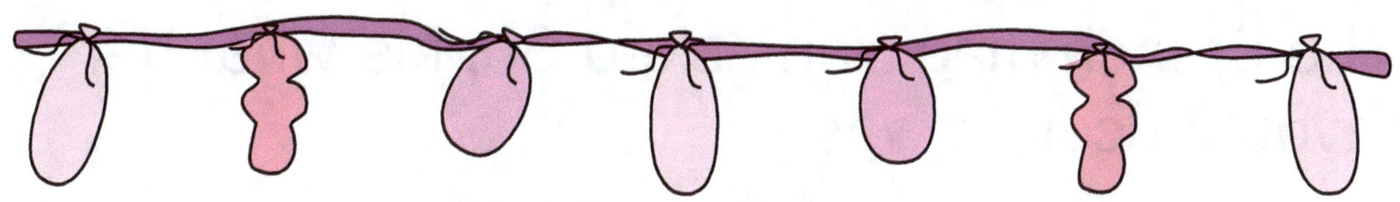

The French magician asked
Sophie how she was:

Sophie was feeling **very good**
as it was her birthday party!
So she replied:

The French magician asked Sophie what her favourite colour was.

Sophie's favourite colour was pink, so she said **rose**. **Rose** is pink in French.

Okay, boys and girls I need your help!
We need to say **rose** three times as we clap.

(Now the magician needs as much help as possible, so if you're reading this story now, please join in too!)

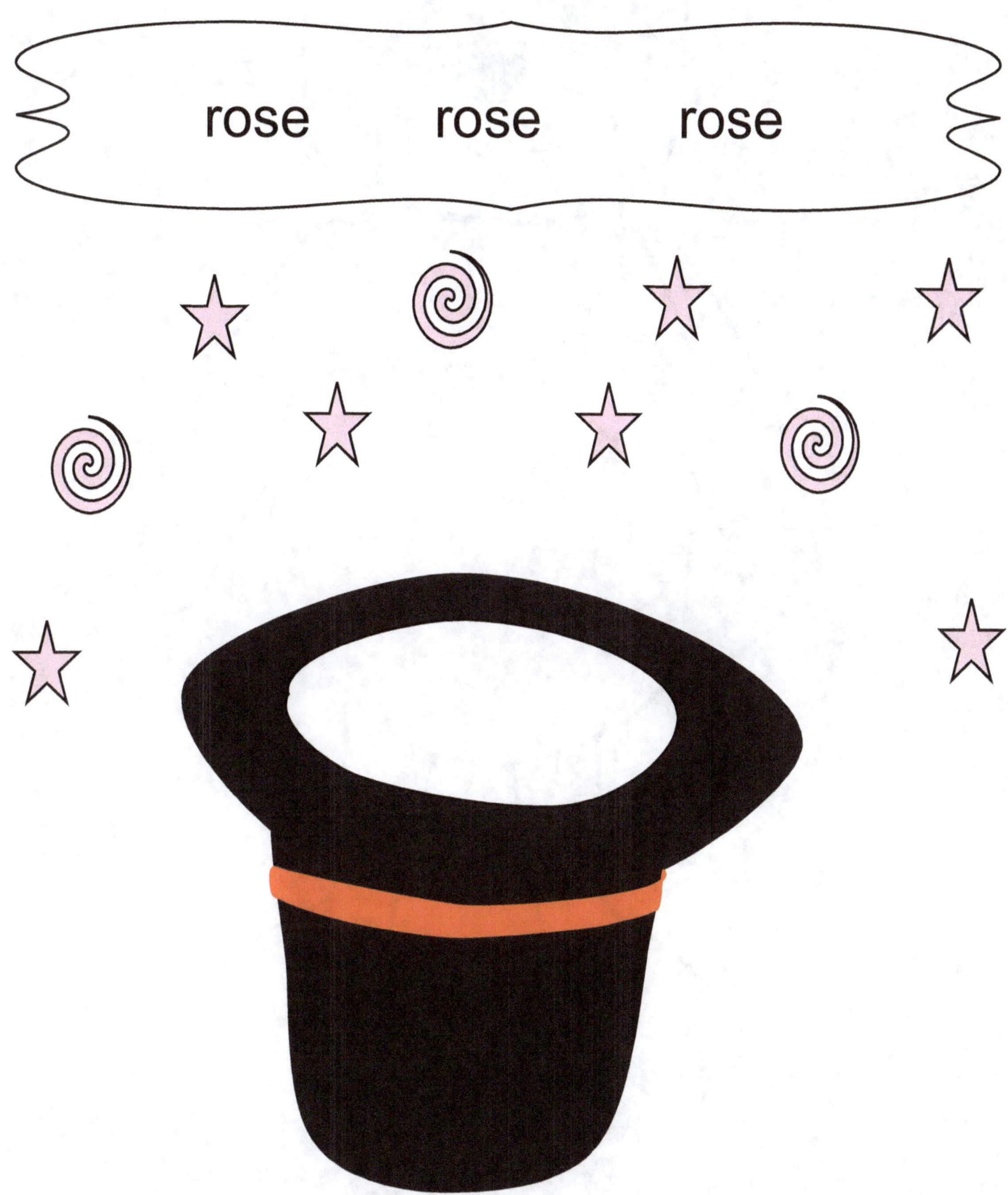

And out of the hat came a teddy that was the colour….

rose

Sophie was so happy that she thanked the magician in French.

Next the magician turned to Sophie's best friend, and he asked:

Sophie's best friend said blue was her favourite colour.

Okay, boys and girls I need your help!
We need to say **bleu** three times as we clap.

(Now the magician needs as much help as possible, so if you're
 reading this story now, please join in too!)

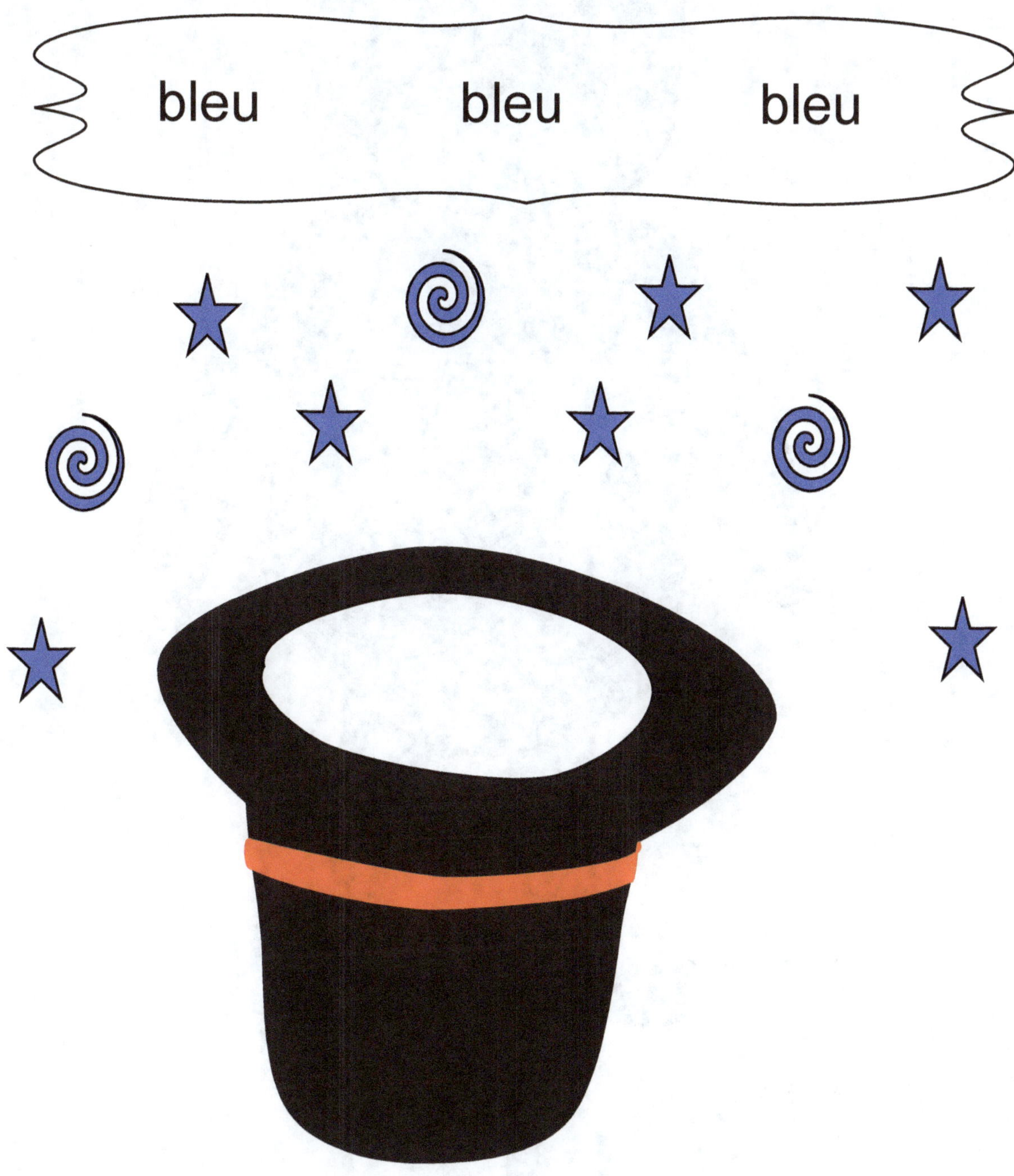

And out of the hat came a teddy that was
the colour….

bleu

Sophie's best friend was so happy that she thanked the magician in French.

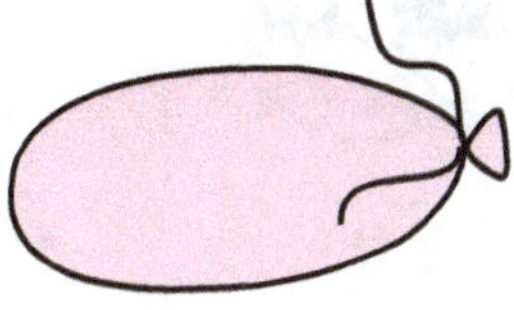

Next the French magician asked a little boy:

The little boy said green
was his favourite colour.

Okay, boys and girls I need your help!
We need to say **vert** three times as we clap.

(Now the magician needs as much help as possible, so if you're reading this story now, please join in too!)

And out of the hat came a teddy that was the colour….

vert

Wow, what a magician!

Out of the hat kept on coming more and more teddies for Sophie's friends!

Eventually EVERYONE had a new teddy!

Can you remember the colours in French for all the new teddies?   Lets say them together!

It had been a wonderful birthday party! The French magician waved goodbye and they all said "**Au revoir**."

Useful French words and phrases

Bonjour …………………………… Hello

Je m'appelle……………………… My name is …

Comment ça va?…………………… How are you?

Ça va très bien ………………… Very well

Merci……………………………… Thank you

Au revoir………………………… Goodbye

un

deux

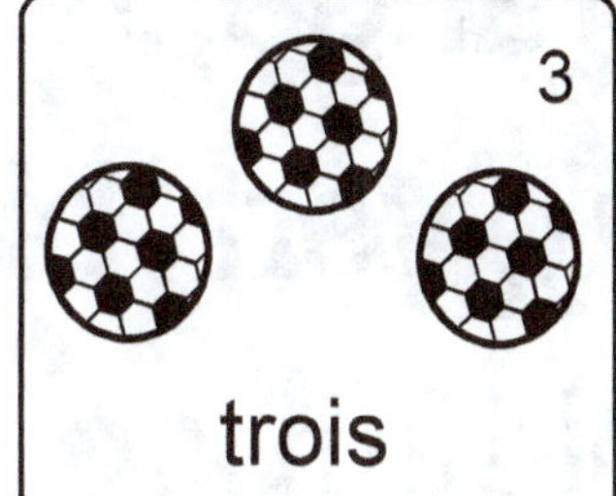

trois

sweets

bonbons

Quel est ton animal préféré?………What is your favourite animal?

a rabbit

un lapin

a bird

un oiseau

a dog

un chien

Quelle est ta couleur préférée?…..What is your favourite colour?

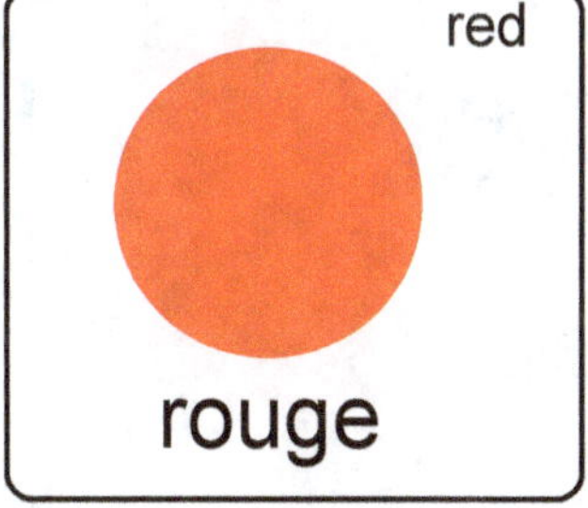

red

rouge

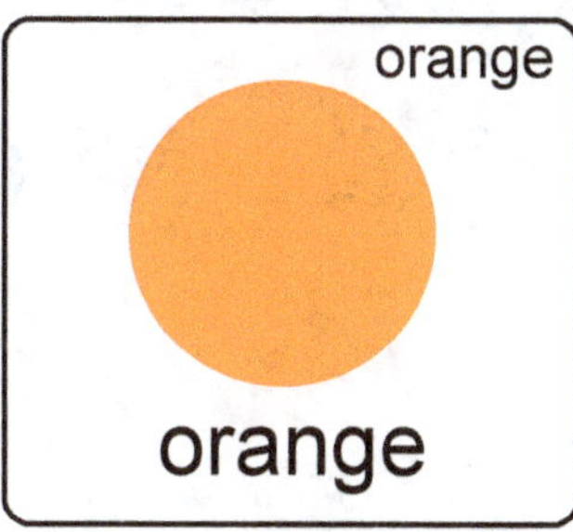

orange

orange

yellow

jaune

green

vert

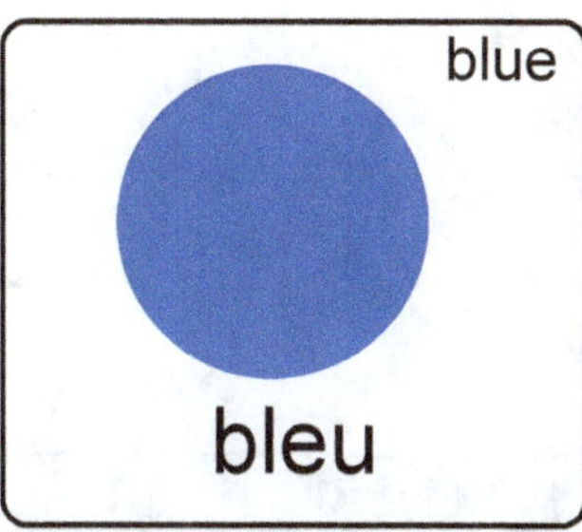

blue

bleu

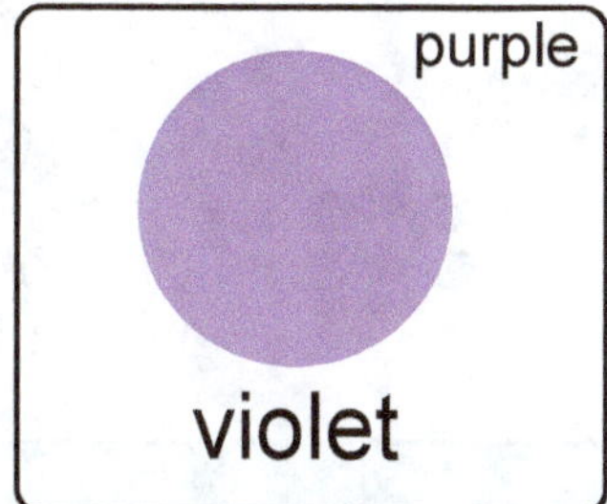

purple

violet

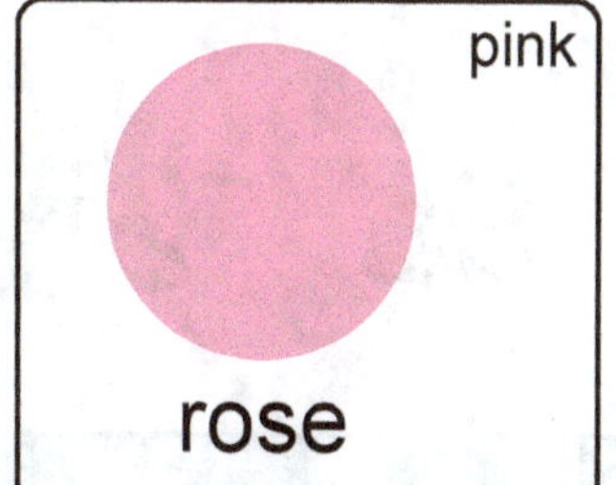

pink

rose

Let's sing a song!

The following words could either be sung to a made up tune, or you could try saying the words as a rap.

For inspiration of a melody to use you could hum first a nursery rhyme. How many different versions can you create using the lyrics?

rouge orange, rouge orange

vert bleu, vert bleu

rose violet, rose violet

jaune, jaune

rouge orange, rouge orange

vert bleu, vert bleu

rose violet, rose violet

jaune, jaune